Copyright © 2023 by Cameron Bailey (Author)

All rights reserved. No part of this book may be reproduced or utilized in any form or by any means, electronic or mechanical, including photocopying, recording or by any information storage and retrieval system, without permission in writing from the publisher, except for brief quotations in critical articles or reviews.

The content of this book is based on various sources and is intended for educational and entertainment purposes only. While the author has made every effort to ensure the accuracy, completeness, and reliability of the information provided, the information may be subject to errors, omissions, or inaccuracies. Therefore, the author makes no warranties, express or implied, regarding the content of this book.

Readers are advised to seek the guidance of a licensed professional before attempting any techniques or actions outlined in this book. The author is not responsible for any losses, damages, or injuries that may arise from the use of information contained within. The information provided in this book is not intended to be a substitute for professional advice, and readers should not rely solely on the information presented.

By reading this book, readers acknowledge that the author is not providing legal, financial, medical, or professional advice. Any reliance on the information contained in this book is solely at the reader's own risk.

Thank you for selecting this book as a valuable source of knowledge and inspiration. Our aim is to provide you with insights and information that will enrich your understanding and enhance your personal growth. We appreciate your decision to embark on this journey of discovery with us, and we hope that this book will exceed your expectations and leave a lasting impact on your life.

Title: Confidence is Key
Subtitle: Practical Exercises for Developing and Strengthening Your Self-Confidence

Series: The Secrets of Self-Confidence: A Comprehensive Guide to Achieving Your Goals
Author: Cameron Bailey

Table of Contents

Introduction 5
  What is self-confidence? 5
  Why is self-confidence important? 7
  How to build your self-confidence 9

Chapter 1: The importance of self-confidence 12
  Self-confidence is essential for a happy and successful life 12
  When you have self-confidence, you are more likely to take risks, achieve your goals, and be happy with your life 14
  There are many things you can do to build your self-confidence 16

Chapter 2: How to build your self-confidence 19
  Identify your self-confidence blocks 19
  Challenge your negative thoughts 22
  Focus on your strengths. Everyone has strengths 25
  Set realistic goals 27
  Take risks 29
  Surround yourself with positive people 31
  Practice positive self-talk. The way you talk to yourself matters 34

Chapter 3: Maintaining your self-confidence 37
  Continue to challenge yourself 37

Be patient *39*

Celebrate your successes *42*

Chapter 4: Dealing with setbacks **45**

Don't give up *45*

Learn from your mistakes *48*

Don't compare yourself to others *51*

Celebrate your successes *55*

Chapter 5: Finding your inner confidence **58**

What is inner confidence? *58*

How to find your inner confidence *60*

Conclusion **63**

The importance of inner confidence *63*

How to continue to build your inner confidence *66*

Wordbook **69**

Supplementary Materials **71**

Introduction
What is self-confidence?

Self-confidence is the belief in oneself and one's abilities. It's a feeling of trust in one's own judgment, abilities, and qualities. People who are self-confident tend to have a positive self-image and are able to face challenges and adversity with a sense of assurance.

Self-confidence is not something that is innate, but rather it is something that can be developed and improved upon with practice. It is not a fixed trait, but rather a skill that can be learned and honed over time.

Self-confidence is closely related to self-esteem and self-worth. Self-esteem is the overall evaluation of oneself, while self-worth is the belief in one's inherent value and worthiness. These three concepts are interconnected and influence one another. A person with high self-worth is likely to have high self-esteem and, in turn, high self-confidence.

Why is self-confidence important?

Self-confidence is essential for a happy and successful life. It allows individuals to take risks and try new things, leading to personal growth and development. With self-confidence, people are more likely to set ambitious goals and pursue them with determination and persistence.

Self-confidence also affects how people interact with others. Those who are self-confident tend to be more assertive, communicate effectively, and form meaningful relationships. They are better equipped to handle criticism and rejection and are less likely to be affected by the opinions of others.

On the other hand, low self-confidence can lead to negative self-talk, self-doubt, and a lack of motivation. It can hold individuals back from achieving their full potential and enjoying life to the fullest. Therefore, building and strengthening one's self-confidence is crucial for personal and professional success.

In the next chapter, we will explore how to build self-confidence through practical exercises and strategies.

Why is self-confidence important?

Self-confidence is a vital ingredient for a happy and successful life. It enables individuals to take risks, face challenges, and pursue their goals with conviction and determination. When people are confident in themselves and their abilities, they are more likely to succeed in their personal and professional endeavors.

Self-confidence impacts every aspect of an individual's life, including their relationships, career, and overall well-being. Here are some of the reasons why self-confidence is so crucial:

1. Improved performance: Self-confidence can boost an individual's performance in various areas of their life. Whether it's sports, academics, or work, people who are confident tend to perform better than those who lack self-confidence. This is because self-confidence helps individuals stay focused, motivated, and committed to their goals.

2. Better relationships: Self-confidence can also enhance one's relationships with others. When people are confident in themselves, they are more likely to communicate effectively, form meaningful connections, and establish healthy boundaries. They are also less likely to be affected by negative opinions and criticisms from others.

3. Greater resilience: Self-confidence enables individuals to bounce back from setbacks and challenges. When people are confident in themselves, they are more resilient and better equipped to handle adversity. They are less likely to give up in the face of obstacles and more likely to keep trying until they succeed.

4. More opportunities: Self-confidence opens up more opportunities for individuals. When people are confident in their abilities, they are more likely to take risks and try new things. This can lead to new opportunities for personal and professional growth and development.

5. Improved well-being: Self-confidence can also contribute to an individual's overall well-being. When people feel good about themselves and their abilities, they are more likely to have positive thoughts and feelings. This, in turn, can lead to improved mental and emotional health.

In summary, self-confidence is essential for personal and professional success. It enables individuals to take risks, face challenges, and pursue their goals with conviction and determination. It also enhances their relationships, resilience, opportunities, and overall well-being. In the next chapter, we will explore how to build self-confidence through practical exercises and strategies.

How to build your self-confidence

Building self-confidence is a process that requires time, effort, and commitment. However, with the right mindset and strategies, anyone can develop and strengthen their self-confidence. In this chapter, we will explore practical exercises and strategies for building self-confidence.

1. Identify your self-confidence blocks

The first step in building self-confidence is to identify the factors that are holding you back. These can be internal factors, such as negative beliefs and self-doubt, or external factors, such as past failures and criticism from others. Once you have identified your self-confidence blocks, you can work on overcoming them.

2. Challenge your negative thoughts

Negative thoughts can undermine your self-confidence and hold you back from achieving your goals. To build self-confidence, it is essential to challenge these negative thoughts and replace them with positive and empowering ones. This can be done by practicing positive self-talk and reframing negative thoughts into positive ones.

3. Focus on your strengths

Everyone has strengths and talents, and focusing on them can boost your self-confidence. Identify your strengths and find ways to use them in your daily life. This can be in your personal or professional life, and can help you feel more confident and capable.

4. Set realistic goals

Setting realistic goals is an important step in building self-confidence. When you set achievable goals, you are more likely to succeed, which can boost your confidence. It is also essential to break down your goals into smaller, manageable steps, which can help you stay motivated and focused.

5. Take risks

Taking risks can be scary, but it is also an essential part of building self-confidence. When you take risks, you challenge yourself and step outside of your comfort zone. This can lead to personal growth and development, which can boost your self-confidence.

6. Surround yourself with positive people

The people you surround yourself with can have a significant impact on your self-confidence. Surrounding yourself with positive and supportive people can boost your confidence and help you feel more capable and empowered.

7. Practice positive self-talk

The way you talk to yourself matters, and practicing positive self-talk can boost your self-confidence. This involves replacing negative self-talk with positive and empowering messages. For example, instead of telling yourself, "I can't do this," tell yourself, "I am capable and will do my best."

In summary, building self-confidence is a process that requires time, effort, and commitment. To build self-confidence, you need to identify your self-confidence blocks, challenge negative thoughts, focus on your strengths, set realistic goals, take risks, surround yourself with positive people, and practice positive self-talk. In the next chapter, we will explore how to maintain your self-confidence and continue to grow and develop.

Chapter 1: The importance of self-confidence
Self-confidence is essential for a happy and successful life

Self-confidence is a crucial factor in living a happy and fulfilling life. When you have self-confidence, you feel more capable, empowered, and in control of your life. In this section, we will explore why self-confidence is essential for a happy and successful life.

1. Self-confidence leads to better decision-making

When you have self-confidence, you are more likely to make better decisions. You trust your judgment and are less likely to second-guess yourself. This can lead to better outcomes and a more fulfilling life.

2. Self-confidence improves relationships

Self-confidence can also improve your relationships with others. When you are confident, you are more likely to communicate effectively and assertively. This can lead to better relationships and more meaningful connections with others.

3. Self-confidence leads to greater resilience

Life is full of challenges and setbacks, but self-confidence can help you overcome them. When you have self-confidence, you are more resilient and better equipped to handle adversity. This can lead to a more fulfilling life, as you are better able to bounce back from setbacks and keep moving forward.

4. Self-confidence leads to greater success

Self-confidence is also crucial for success. When you have self-confidence, you are more likely to take risks, pursue your goals, and achieve success. This can lead to a more fulfilling life, as you are able to accomplish your dreams and live up to your potential.

5. Self-confidence leads to greater happiness

Ultimately, self-confidence leads to greater happiness. When you have self-confidence, you feel more fulfilled, empowered, and in control of your life. This can lead to greater happiness and a more positive outlook on life.

In summary, self-confidence is essential for a happy and successful life. When you have self-confidence, you are more likely to make better decisions, improve your relationships, be more resilient, achieve success, and experience greater happiness. In the next section, we will explore practical strategies for building self-confidence.

When you have self-confidence, you are more likely to take risks, achieve your goals, and be happy with your life

Self-confidence is crucial for achieving success and happiness in life. When you have self-confidence, you feel empowered, capable, and in control of your life. In this section, we will explore why self-confidence is essential for taking risks, achieving goals, and living a happy life.

1. Self-confidence leads to taking risks

When you have self-confidence, you are more likely to take risks. This is because you trust yourself and believe in your abilities. Taking risks is essential for personal and professional growth, and self-confidence is what gives you the courage to take those risks.

2. Self-confidence leads to achieving goals

Self-confidence is also crucial for achieving your goals. When you have self-confidence, you believe in your ability to succeed, and you are more likely to take action towards achieving your goals. You are more likely to persist in the face of obstacles and setbacks, and to keep pushing towards your goals until you achieve them.

3. Self-confidence leads to a happier life

Ultimately, self-confidence leads to a happier life. When you have self-confidence, you feel more fulfilled and empowered, and you are more likely to pursue your passions and interests. This can lead to greater happiness and fulfillment in life.

4. Self-confidence helps you bounce back from setbacks

Another benefit of self-confidence is that it helps you bounce back from setbacks. When you have self-confidence, you are better able to handle failure and rejection. You are more likely to see setbacks as opportunities for growth and learning, rather than as a reflection of your worth or ability.

5. Self-confidence helps you cope with uncertainty

Self-confidence also helps you cope with uncertainty. When you have self-confidence, you are better able to handle situations that are outside of your comfort zone. You are more likely to see uncertainty as an opportunity for growth and adventure, rather than as something to fear.

In summary, self-confidence is essential for taking risks, achieving goals, and living a happy life. When you have self-confidence, you are more likely to take action towards achieving your goals, to bounce back from setbacks, and to cope with uncertainty. In the next section, we will explore practical strategies for building self-confidence.

There are many things you can do to build your self-confidence

Self-confidence is not something that you are born with, but rather it is a skill that can be developed and strengthened over time. There are many things that you can do to build your self-confidence, from developing a positive mindset to taking risks and stepping outside of your comfort zone. In this section, we will explore some practical strategies for building self-confidence.

1. Develop a positive mindset

One of the most important things you can do to build your self-confidence is to develop a positive mindset. This means learning to focus on your strengths, rather than your weaknesses, and practicing positive self-talk. Instead of criticizing yourself or focusing on your flaws, focus on the things that you do well and the positive aspects of yourself. Remind yourself of your accomplishments and celebrate your successes, no matter how small they may seem.

2. Set realistic goals

Setting realistic goals is another key strategy for building self-confidence. When you set goals that are achievable, you are more likely to feel a sense of accomplishment and build confidence in your abilities. Start by setting small, achievable goals and gradually work your way up to more challenging goals. Remember that setbacks and failures are a normal part of the process, so be patient with yourself and celebrate your progress along the way.

3. Take risks and step outside of your comfort zone

Taking risks and stepping outside of your comfort zone is another important strategy for building self-confidence. This means pushing yourself to try new things, even if they are scary or intimidating. When you take risks and try new things, you challenge yourself and build confidence in your abilities. Remember that it's okay to fail and make mistakes along the way – it's all part of the learning process.

4. Practice self-care

Taking care of yourself is also crucial for building self-confidence. This means making time for self-care activities, such as exercise, meditation, or spending time with loved ones. When you prioritize your well-being, you feel more confident and capable of handling challenges that come your way.

5. Surround yourself with positive people

Finally, surrounding yourself with positive people is also important for building self-confidence. When you surround yourself with people who support and encourage you, you feel more confident and empowered. Seek out friends and mentors who believe in you and who will lift you up when you're feeling down.

In summary, building self-confidence is a skill that can be developed and strengthened over time. By developing a positive mindset, setting realistic goals, taking risks, practicing self-care, and surrounding yourself with positive people, you can build confidence in yourself and your abilities. In the next chapter, we will explore specific strategies for building self-confidence in different areas of your life.

Chapter 2: How to build your self-confidence
Identify your self-confidence blocks

Self-confidence blocks are the negative thoughts, beliefs, or experiences that hold us back from building our confidence. They can stem from childhood experiences, societal pressures, or our own self-doubt. However, identifying these blocks is the first step towards overcoming them and building our self-confidence. Here are some strategies for identifying your self-confidence blocks:

1. Journaling

Journaling is a powerful tool for self-reflection and self-discovery. Start by writing down your thoughts and feelings about yourself, your abilities, and your accomplishments. Notice any patterns or recurring themes that emerge. Do you tend to focus on your weaknesses rather than your strengths? Do you often compare yourself to others? Are you afraid of failure or rejection? These can all be signs of self-confidence blocks.

2. Reflect on past experiences

Think back to times when you may have experienced a setback or failure. How did it affect your confidence? Did it cause you to doubt your abilities or question your worth? Reflect on how these experiences have shaped your self-image and identify any negative beliefs that may have resulted from them.

3. Seek feedback from others

Sometimes, our self-confidence blocks are not immediately apparent to us. Seeking feedback from trusted friends or family members can provide valuable insight into areas where we may be holding ourselves back. Ask for honest feedback about your strengths and weaknesses, and any areas where they think you could improve your self-confidence.

4. Pay attention to negative self-talk

Negative self-talk is one of the most common self-confidence blocks. It can be the voice in our head that tells us we're not good enough, or that we'll never succeed. Pay attention to your self-talk and notice when it becomes negative. Challenge those thoughts by asking yourself if they're really true, or if there's another way to look at the situation.

5. Consider seeking professional help

If you're having trouble identifying your self-confidence blocks, or if you're struggling to overcome them on your own, consider seeking the help of a professional therapist or counselor. They can provide guidance and support as you work to identify and overcome your self-confidence blocks, and help you develop strategies for building your self-confidence.

By identifying and overcoming our self-confidence blocks, we can begin to build a stronger sense of self-confidence and move towards achieving our goals and living a happier, more fulfilling life.

Challenge your negative thoughts

Negative thoughts are a major obstacle to building self-confidence. They can prevent you from taking action and achieving your goals. Therefore, it is essential to challenge these negative thoughts and replace them with positive ones. In this section, we will discuss some strategies for challenging negative thoughts.

1. Identify Your Negative Thoughts

The first step in challenging negative thoughts is to identify them. Negative thoughts can be automatic, and you may not even be aware of them. Therefore, it is essential to pay attention to your thoughts and identify the ones that are negative. Some examples of negative thoughts include:

- "I'm not good enough"
- "I'm not smart enough"
- "I always mess things up"
- "I'm a failure"
- "Nobody likes me"

2. Examine the Evidence

Once you have identified your negative thoughts, the next step is to examine the evidence for and against them. For example, if you think, "I'm not good enough," ask yourself, "What evidence do I have to support this thought? What evidence do I have against it?" You may find that there is little evidence to support your negative thought and that there is more evidence to contradict it.

3. Challenge Your Thinking Errors

Thinking errors, also known as cognitive distortions, are common patterns of thinking that can lead to negative thoughts. There are several types of thinking errors, including all-or-nothing thinking, overgeneralization, and catastrophizing. For example, all-or-nothing thinking is the belief that things are either all good or all bad, with no middle ground. To challenge this thinking error, try to find shades of gray in situations and focus on the positives.

4. Practice Positive Self-Talk

Positive self-talk is a powerful tool for challenging negative thoughts. Replace negative thoughts with positive ones by reframing them in a positive way. For example, if you think, "I always mess things up," replace it with, "I may make mistakes, but I also learn from them and improve."

5. Use Affirmations

Affirmations are positive statements that you can repeat to yourself to build your self-confidence. For example, "I am confident and capable" or "I can achieve my goals." Repeat these affirmations to yourself daily, especially when you are feeling down or insecure.

6. Seek Support

It can be challenging to challenge negative thoughts on your own. Seek support from friends, family, or a therapist. They can provide a fresh perspective and help you challenge your negative thoughts.

In conclusion, challenging negative thoughts is an essential step in building self-confidence. By identifying your negative thoughts, examining the evidence, challenging thinking errors, practicing positive self-talk, using affirmations, and seeking support, you can replace negative thoughts with positive ones and build your self-confidence.

Focus on your strengths. Everyone has strengths

When it comes to building self-confidence, one of the most effective ways is to focus on your strengths. Everyone has strengths, even if they don't realize it. By identifying and utilizing your strengths, you can increase your confidence and improve your overall sense of self-worth. In this section, we'll explore some tips and strategies for identifying and focusing on your strengths.

1. Identify your strengths The first step in focusing on your strengths is to identify them. Think about the things that come easily to you, or the activities that you enjoy doing. Consider what others have complimented you on in the past. These are all potential strengths that you can focus on. Make a list of your strengths, and keep it handy as a reminder of the things that you do well.

2. Utilize your strengths Once you've identified your strengths, find ways to utilize them in your daily life. Look for opportunities to use your strengths at work or in your hobbies. If you're good at public speaking, for example, look for opportunities to speak in front of others. If you're creative, find ways to incorporate your creativity into your daily activities. The more you use your strengths, the more confident you'll become.

3. Develop new strengths While it's important to focus on your existing strengths, it's also beneficial to develop new ones. Think about areas where you'd like to improve, or skills that you'd like to acquire. Set goals for yourself and work towards achieving them. By developing new strengths, you'll not only increase your self-confidence, but you'll also expand your horizons and open up new opportunities for yourself.

4. Don't compare yourself to others When focusing on your strengths, it's important to remember not to compare yourself to others. Everyone has their own unique strengths and weaknesses, and it's not productive to compare yourself to someone else. Instead, focus on your own progress and celebrate your own accomplishments.

5. Practice gratitude Finally, practicing gratitude can help you to focus on your strengths and build your self-confidence. Take time each day to think about the things that you're grateful for, including your strengths and accomplishments. By focusing on the positive aspects of your life, you'll feel more confident and self-assured.

In conclusion, focusing on your strengths is a powerful way to build your self-confidence. By identifying and utilizing your strengths, developing new ones, avoiding comparisons, and practicing gratitude, you can increase your confidence and improve your overall sense of well-being.

Set realistic goals

Setting realistic goals is an essential step towards building self-confidence. When we set realistic goals for ourselves, we create a roadmap that we can follow to achieve our desired outcomes. Here are some tips on how to set realistic goals:

1. Identify your goals: The first step in setting realistic goals is to identify what you want to achieve. Start by brainstorming a list of goals, and then narrow them down to the most important ones. Focus on goals that are meaningful and aligned with your values.

2. Be specific: Once you have identified your goals, make them as specific as possible. Instead of setting a vague goal like "get in shape," set a specific goal like "lose 10 pounds in the next three months."

3. Make them measurable: A measurable goal is one that you can track your progress towards. For example, if your goal is to save money, you can measure your progress by tracking how much you save each week.

4. Break them down into smaller steps: Big goals can be overwhelming, so it's important to break them down into smaller, more manageable steps. This will make it easier to stay motivated and on track.

5. Be realistic: When setting goals, it's important to be realistic about what you can achieve. Setting goals that are too ambitious can be discouraging if you don't achieve them. Consider your current resources, skills, and time when setting your goals.

6. Set deadlines: Setting deadlines for your goals can help you stay motivated and focused. Make sure your deadlines are realistic and achievable.

7. Celebrate your progress: Celebrating your progress towards your goals can help keep you motivated and build your self-confidence. Set up small rewards for yourself along the way.

Setting realistic goals is a key part of building self-confidence. By setting goals that are specific, measurable, and achievable, you can create a roadmap that will help you achieve your desired outcomes. Remember to celebrate your progress along the way, and don't be afraid to adjust your goals as needed. With persistence and effort, you can achieve anything you set your mind to.

Take risks

Taking risks is an essential aspect of building self-confidence. It can help you overcome fear and develop a stronger sense of self-esteem. Here are some strategies for taking risks and building self-confidence:

1. Define your goals: Before you take a risk, it's essential to identify your goals and what you hope to achieve. Define your goals clearly, and make sure they align with your values and passions. This will help you make informed decisions about the risks you take.

2. Start small: Taking small risks can help you build confidence gradually. Start by doing something that feels slightly outside your comfort zone. For example, if you're afraid of public speaking, start by speaking up in small groups and then gradually move on to larger audiences.

3. Visualize success: Visualization can be a powerful tool for building confidence. Before taking a risk, visualize yourself succeeding and achieving your goals. This can help reduce anxiety and boost your confidence.

4. Embrace failure: Failure is a natural part of taking risks, and it's important to embrace it as a learning opportunity. Rather than viewing failure as a personal reflection of your abilities, use it as an opportunity to learn and grow.

5. Seek support: Taking risks can be challenging, and it's important to have a support system in place. Surround yourself with positive, supportive people who believe in you and your goals.

6. Celebrate successes: Celebrating your successes, no matter how small, can help you build confidence and reinforce positive behavior. Take time to acknowledge and celebrate your achievements, and use them as motivation to continue taking risks and building self-confidence.

By taking calculated risks, setting clear goals, and embracing failure as a learning opportunity, you can develop the confidence you need to achieve your goals and live a fulfilling life.

Surround yourself with positive people

We are social creatures and we need other people to support and encourage us. That's why it's important to surround yourself with positive people if you want to build your self-confidence. The people we surround ourselves with can have a huge impact on our thoughts, feelings, and behaviors. Here are some ways that positive people can help you boost your self-confidence:

1. Positive people provide encouragement and support

When you are trying to build your self-confidence, it's important to have people in your life who believe in you and encourage you. Positive people can provide this kind of support. They can cheer you on when you succeed and pick you up when you fail. This kind of encouragement can help you stay motivated and focused on your goals.

2. Positive people help you see the good in yourself

Sometimes it's hard to see the good in ourselves. We focus on our weaknesses and flaws instead of our strengths and accomplishments. Positive people can help us see the good in ourselves. They can remind us of our strengths, achievements, and positive qualities. This kind of feedback can help us build our self-confidence and feel better about ourselves.

3. Positive people challenge you to be your best self

Positive people want the best for you. They want you to be happy, successful, and fulfilled. That's why they will challenge you to be your best self. They will push you out of your comfort zone, encourage you to take risks, and support you as you grow and develop. This kind of challenge can help you build your self-confidence by showing you what you are capable of.

4. Positive people are good role models

When we see other people succeeding and being happy, it can be inspiring. Positive people can be good role models for us. They can show us what it looks like to be confident, resilient, and successful. This kind of modeling can help us build our self-confidence by giving us a blueprint for how to achieve our goals.

5. Positive people create a positive atmosphere

Positive people create a positive atmosphere wherever they go. They are upbeat, optimistic, and energetic. When you are around positive people, it's hard to feel down or discouraged. This kind of atmosphere can help you build your self-confidence by lifting your mood and giving you a sense of hope and optimism.

In conclusion, surrounding yourself with positive people is a great way to boost your self-confidence. Positive people can provide encouragement, support, and challenge.

They can help you see the good in yourself and give you a blueprint for success. They can also create a positive atmosphere that lifts your mood and gives you a sense of hope and optimism. So, if you want to build your self-confidence, start by surrounding yourself with positive people.

Practice positive self-talk. The way you talk to yourself matters

Practicing positive self-talk is an essential step in building your self-confidence. The way you talk to yourself can have a significant impact on your thoughts, feelings, and behavior. Negative self-talk can create self-doubt, anxiety, and insecurity, while positive self-talk can help you feel more confident, motivated, and optimistic.

Here are some strategies you can use to practice positive self-talk:

1. Identify negative self-talk patterns: The first step in practicing positive self-talk is to become aware of your negative self-talk patterns. This could involve paying attention to your inner dialogue and the things you say to yourself when faced with challenging situations. You may notice that you tend to criticize yourself or doubt your abilities.

2. Challenge negative self-talk: Once you have identified your negative self-talk patterns, challenge them. Ask yourself whether these thoughts are based on reality or whether they are just assumptions or fears. Try to find evidence that supports more positive thoughts and beliefs.

3. Use positive affirmations: Positive affirmations are short, powerful statements that can help you overcome

negative self-talk. They are usually positive, present-tense statements that affirm your strengths and abilities. For example, you might say, "I am confident in my abilities," "I trust myself to make the right decisions," or "I am worthy of success."

4. Reframe negative thoughts: Reframing involves changing the way you think about a situation. Instead of focusing on the negative aspects, try to find the positives. For example, instead of saying, "I'm never going to be good at this," you could say, "I'm still learning, and I can improve with practice."

5. Practice gratitude: Gratitude is a powerful way to shift your focus from negative to positive. When you are feeling down, take a moment to think about the things you are grateful for in your life. This could be as simple as appreciating the sunshine or the support of a loved one.

6. Visualize success: Visualization involves imagining yourself succeeding in a particular situation. This can help you build confidence and reduce anxiety. For example, if you are nervous about a job interview, try visualizing yourself answering the questions confidently and impressing the interviewer.

7. Celebrate your successes: Finally, it is important to celebrate your successes, no matter how small they may be.

This helps you build momentum and reinforces positive self-talk. Take the time to acknowledge your accomplishments and give yourself credit for your hard work and dedication.

In conclusion, practicing positive self-talk is a crucial part of building self-confidence. By identifying and challenging negative self-talk patterns, using positive affirmations, reframing negative thoughts, practicing gratitude, visualizing success, and celebrating your successes, you can cultivate a more positive and confident mindset. With time and practice, these strategies can help you build lasting self-confidence and achieve your goals.

Chapter 3: Maintaining your self-confidence
Continue to challenge yourself

Once you have worked on building your self-confidence, it's important to maintain it by continuing to challenge yourself. When you challenge yourself, you put yourself in new and sometimes uncomfortable situations, which can help you to grow and develop even more self-confidence.

Here are some ways to continue to challenge yourself:

1. Set new goals: Once you achieve a goal, set a new one that is slightly more challenging. This will help you to continue to push yourself and grow.

2. Try new things: Whether it's a new hobby, a new skill, or a new experience, trying new things can help you to step out of your comfort zone and gain new experiences.

3. Step up in your career: Take on new responsibilities or projects at work that challenge you and push you to learn and grow.

4. Take on a leadership role: Leading a team or group can be challenging, but it can also help you to develop important skills like communication and decision-making.

5. Push through fear: When faced with a situation that scares you, try to push through the fear and take action. This

can be as simple as speaking up in a meeting or as bold as starting your own business.

6. Travel: Traveling to new places can be a great way to challenge yourself and gain new experiences. It can also help you to develop important skills like adaptability and problem-solving.

Remember, challenging yourself doesn't always mean taking huge risks or making drastic changes. It can be as simple as trying something new or taking a small step outside of your comfort zone. The key is to keep pushing yourself to grow and develop your self-confidence.

Be patient

Self-confidence is not something that you can build overnight. It takes time, effort, and patience. While it is important to have a sense of urgency when it comes to building your self-confidence, it is also important to be patient with yourself.

It is easy to get discouraged when you don't see results immediately, but it is important to remember that building self-confidence is a process. It requires a lot of effort and dedication on your part, but the end result is well worth it. Here are some tips on how to be patient while building your self-confidence:

1. Recognize that building self-confidence is a journey, not a destination: The process of building self-confidence is ongoing. It's not something that you can achieve and then forget about. It requires continuous effort and attention.

2. Celebrate small successes: It's important to celebrate small successes along the way. Recognize and acknowledge the progress that you are making, no matter how small it may be. Celebrating your successes will help keep you motivated and on track.

3. Don't compare yourself to others: It's easy to get discouraged when you compare yourself to others who may appear more self-confident than you. Remember that

everyone has their own journey and that you are making progress at your own pace.

4. Set realistic expectations: Be realistic about the progress that you can make in a given time frame. Setting unrealistic expectations will only lead to disappointment and frustration.

5. Be kind to yourself: Don't be too hard on yourself. Building self-confidence takes time, and it's okay to make mistakes along the way. Treat yourself with kindness and compassion.

6. Surround yourself with supportive people: Surrounding yourself with people who support and encourage you can make a big difference in your self-confidence journey. Having a support system can help you stay motivated and positive.

7. Practice self-care: Taking care of yourself is an important part of building self-confidence. Make time for activities that you enjoy, eat well, exercise regularly, and get enough rest.

8. Keep a positive attitude: A positive attitude can make all the difference in your self-confidence journey. Focus on the progress that you are making, and don't dwell on setbacks.

9. Seek professional help: If you are struggling to build your self-confidence, don't be afraid to seek professional help. A therapist or counselor can help you work through any underlying issues that may be holding you back.

In conclusion, building self-confidence takes time and effort, but it is well worth it. Being patient with yourself and recognizing the progress that you are making can help you stay motivated and on track. Remember to celebrate your successes along the way, and don't be afraid to seek professional help if you need it. With dedication and perseverance, you can build the self-confidence that you need to achieve your goals and live your best life.

Celebrate your successes

Building self-confidence is not a one-time event, but a continuous process. As you work on building your self-confidence, it's important to acknowledge and celebrate your successes, no matter how small they may seem. Celebrating your successes can help you maintain your self-confidence, stay motivated, and continue to work towards your goals.

Here are some ways you can celebrate your successes and maintain your self-confidence:

1. Reflect on Your Achievements

When you achieve something, take time to reflect on your accomplishment. Consider the hard work and dedication that went into achieving your goal, and acknowledge the progress you have made. This reflection can help you appreciate your successes and feel proud of what you have accomplished.

2. Reward Yourself

After achieving a goal, it's important to reward yourself for your hard work. Treat yourself to something you enjoy, whether it's a special meal, a movie, or a day off. This can help you feel good about your accomplishments and motivate you to continue working towards your goals.

3. Share Your Successes

Sharing your successes with others can be a great way to celebrate and maintain your self-confidence. Talk to a friend, family member, or colleague about your achievements and how you accomplished them. Their positive feedback and support can help reinforce your confidence and inspire you to continue working towards your goals.

4. Keep a Journal

Keeping a journal of your successes and achievements can be a powerful tool to maintain your self-confidence. Write down your goals, accomplishments, and the steps you took to achieve them. When you're feeling discouraged or doubting your abilities, you can revisit your journal and remind yourself of your accomplishments and the progress you have made.

5. Set New Goals

After achieving a goal, it's important to set new ones to continue challenging yourself and maintaining your self-confidence. Set new goals that are challenging but attainable, and break them down into smaller, manageable steps. Celebrate each milestone you reach on the way to achieving your new goal.

6. Embrace Failure

It's important to remember that failure is a natural part of the learning process. Don't be discouraged by setbacks or failures. Instead, use them as an opportunity to learn and grow. Analyze what went wrong, and what you can do differently next time. Embracing failure can help you maintain your self-confidence by reminding you that setbacks are not a reflection of your abilities.

7. Practice Gratitude

Maintaining a positive attitude can help you maintain your self-confidence. Take time to practice gratitude by reflecting on the things you are grateful for in your life. This can help shift your focus away from negative thoughts and reinforce your self-confidence.

In conclusion, celebrating your successes is an important aspect of maintaining your self-confidence. Reflecting on your achievements, rewarding yourself, sharing your successes, keeping a journal, setting new goals, embracing failure, and practicing gratitude are all effective ways to celebrate your successes and maintain your self-confidence. Remember, building self-confidence is a continuous process, and celebrating your successes can help you stay motivated and focused on your goals.

Chapter 4: Dealing with setbacks
Don't give up

Dealing with setbacks is an essential part of building and maintaining self-confidence. Setbacks can come in many forms, such as failures, rejections, criticisms, and unexpected changes. However, what sets successful and confident people apart from others is not the absence of setbacks, but their ability to bounce back and keep going despite them.

Here are some tips on how to deal with setbacks and not give up on your goals and dreams:

1. Embrace failure as a learning opportunity. Many successful people attribute their achievements to the lessons they learned from their failures. Instead of seeing failure as a sign of weakness or incompetence, see it as a chance to gain new insights, perspectives, and skills. Reflect on what went wrong, what you could have done differently, and what you can do better next time.

2. Focus on your strengths and achievements. When you encounter setbacks, it's easy to fall into a negative spiral of self-doubt and self-blame. However, this will only make things worse. Instead, remind yourself of your strengths, accomplishments, and positive qualities. Write them down, and read them whenever you feel discouraged. This will help you maintain a sense of perspective and self-worth.

3. Seek support and feedback from others. It's okay to ask for help and advice when you're facing challenges. Talk to your friends, family, mentors, or colleagues, and share your struggles and concerns. They may offer you new insights, encouragement, or practical solutions that you haven't considered before. Also, ask for feedback on your performance or progress, and use it constructively to improve.

4. Practice self-care and stress management. Setbacks can be stressful and draining, both physically and emotionally. Therefore, it's crucial to take care of yourself and manage your stress levels. This includes getting enough sleep, exercise, healthy food, and relaxation time. Also, try to avoid self-medicating with alcohol, drugs, or other unhealthy habits, as they can make the situation worse.

5. Stay focused on your long-term goals and vision. Setbacks can make you lose sight of your purpose and motivation. However, it's important to keep your eyes on the prize and remind yourself of your big picture goals and vision. Visualize your success, and create a plan to get there. Break your goals down into smaller, achievable steps, and celebrate each milestone along the way.

6. Learn to manage your emotions and reactions. Setbacks can trigger strong emotions such as anger,

frustration, disappointment, or sadness. It's natural to feel them, but it's essential to manage them effectively. Avoid lashing out at others, blaming yourself, or giving up altogether. Instead, try to express your feelings in a constructive way, such as journaling, talking to a therapist, or engaging in a creative activity.

7. Keep learning and growing. Finally, don't let setbacks discourage you from pursuing your personal and professional growth. Instead, use them as a catalyst for learning and development. Take courses, read books, attend seminars, or seek mentorship opportunities that can help you acquire new skills, expand your knowledge, and broaden your horizons. This will not only help you build your self-confidence, but also increase your resilience, adaptability, and flexibility.

In conclusion, setbacks are inevitable in life, but they don't have to define your self-worth or your future. By adopting a growth mindset, seeking support, staying focused on your goals, and managing your emotions effectively, you can overcome setbacks and emerge stronger and more confident than ever before. Remember, the most successful people in the world are not those who never fail, but those who never give up.

Learn from your mistakes

Learning from your mistakes is an essential part of building and maintaining self-confidence. Nobody is perfect, and setbacks are a natural part of life. However, it's how you handle those setbacks that will determine your ability to succeed in the future. Here are some strategies for learning from your mistakes and using them to build your self-confidence.

1. Don't dwell on the mistake.

When you make a mistake, it's natural to feel frustrated, disappointed, or even angry. However, dwelling on your mistake will only make you feel worse and prevent you from moving forward. Instead, try to acknowledge your mistake, accept responsibility for it, and then focus on finding a solution.

2. Analyze the mistake.

Once you've acknowledged your mistake, take some time to analyze what went wrong. Try to identify the root cause of the problem and figure out what you could have done differently. This will help you avoid making the same mistake in the future and give you a sense of control over the situation.

3. Look for the positive.

Even when things don't go as planned, there is usually something positive that can be taken from the situation. Try to focus on the lessons you've learned and the progress you've made, rather than the setback itself. This will help you maintain a positive attitude and build your self-confidence.

4. Use your mistakes to set new goals.

When you experience a setback, it's an opportunity to reassess your goals and make adjustments as needed. Use your mistakes as a learning experience and set new, achievable goals for yourself. This will give you something positive to focus on and help you regain your sense of direction.

5. Take action.

Once you've analyzed your mistake and set new goals, it's time to take action. Don't be afraid to try new things or take calculated risks. Use your mistakes as a stepping stone to your success, rather than a roadblock.

6. Seek feedback.

Getting feedback from others can be an invaluable tool for learning from your mistakes. Ask friends, family members, or colleagues for their honest opinions about what went wrong and what you could have done differently. This will help you gain new perspectives and insights, and improve your skills for the future.

7. Practice self-compassion.

Remember that making mistakes is a natural part of the learning process. Don't be too hard on yourself, and practice self-compassion. Treat yourself with kindness and understanding, and recognize that mistakes are an opportunity for growth and improvement.

In conclusion, learning from your mistakes is an essential part of building and maintaining self-confidence. By analyzing your mistakes, looking for the positive, setting new goals, taking action, seeking feedback, and practicing self-compassion, you can turn setbacks into opportunities for growth and success.

Don't compare yourself to others

Introduction: One of the most common pitfalls in building self-confidence is comparing yourself to others. It's a natural tendency to measure ourselves against others, but it can be destructive if it leads to negative self-talk and a lack of self-esteem. In this chapter, we'll explore why comparing ourselves to others is harmful, and how we can break the habit and develop a healthier self-image.

Why Comparing Yourself to Others is Harmful: There are several reasons why comparing yourself to others is harmful:

1. You're Comparing Apples to Oranges: Comparing yourself to others is often unfair because you're comparing different people with different circumstances, experiences, and abilities. It's like comparing apples to oranges. We all have unique strengths and weaknesses, and comparing ourselves to others can lead to unrealistic expectations and feelings of inadequacy.

2. It Leads to Negative Self-Talk: When you compare yourself to others, you may find yourself engaging in negative self-talk. You might think, "I'll never be as good as them," or "I'm not talented enough to do that." This kind of self-talk can be damaging to your self-esteem and can lead to a lack of motivation and confidence.

3. It Can Stifle Creativity: When you're focused on comparing yourself to others, you may limit your creativity and originality. You may try to emulate others instead of finding your unique style and voice. This can limit your potential and prevent you from reaching your full potential.

4. It Can be a Distraction: Comparing yourself to others can be a distraction from your own goals and priorities. It can take away from the time and energy you need to focus on your own growth and development. Instead of worrying about what others are doing, focus on your own progress and celebrate your achievements.

How to Stop Comparing Yourself to Others:

1. Recognize Your Triggers: The first step in breaking the habit of comparing yourself to others is to recognize your triggers. What situations or people tend to trigger feelings of inadequacy or self-doubt? Once you identify these triggers, you can take steps to avoid them or manage them more effectively.

2. Focus on Your Own Goals and Progress: Instead of comparing yourself to others, focus on your own goals and progress. Set realistic goals for yourself and track your progress. Celebrate your successes and learn from your mistakes. When you focus on your own journey, you'll be less likely to compare yourself to others.

3. Practice Gratitude: Gratitude is a powerful tool for boosting self-esteem and reducing negative self-talk. Take time each day to reflect on the things you're grateful for in your life. This can help shift your focus from what you don't have to what you do have.

4. Surround Yourself with Positive People: Surrounding yourself with positive, supportive people can help you break the habit of comparing yourself to others. Seek out friends and mentors who are supportive and encouraging. Avoid people who are negative or critical of you.

5. Be Mindful of Your Social Media Use: Social media can be a breeding ground for comparison and negative self-talk. Be mindful of how much time you're spending on social media and how it's affecting your mood and self-esteem. Consider taking a break from social media or limiting your use.

Comparing yourself to others is a habit that can be difficult to break, but it's essential for building self-confidence and a healthy self-image. By recognizing your triggers, focusing on your own goals and progress, practicing gratitude, surrounding yourself with positive people, and being mindful of your social media use, you can break the habit and develop a healthier perspective on yourself and your abilities. Remember, you are unique, and your journey is your own. Embrace it and celebrate your achievements along the way.

In conclusion, building self-confidence is an ongoing process that requires effort, dedication, and patience. It's essential for achieving our goals and living a happy, fulfilled life. We all have the power to improve our self-confidence, regardless of our background, experiences, or past failures. By identifying our self-confidence blocks, challenging negative thoughts, focusing on our strengths, setting realistic goals, taking risks, surrounding ourselves with positive people, and practicing positive self-talk, we can build our self-confidence and maintain it in the face of setbacks. Remember, self-confidence is not about being perfect or better than others, but about believing in ourselves and our abilities. With persistence and determination, we can overcome our fears, achieve our dreams, and become the best version of ourselves.

Celebrate your successes

Celebrating your successes is an essential aspect of building and maintaining self-confidence. Whether it's a big achievement or a small one, taking the time to recognize and celebrate your successes can have a significant impact on your self-esteem and overall well-being.

One of the main reasons why celebrating your successes is so important is that it helps you to acknowledge your progress and recognize your accomplishments. When you're working towards a goal, it's easy to get caught up in the day-to-day challenges and forget how far you've come. By taking the time to celebrate your successes, you're giving yourself the opportunity to reflect on your journey and appreciate the hard work and effort you've put in to get to where you are.

Celebrating your successes can also help to boost your self-confidence by reminding you of your abilities and strengths. When you achieve something that you've been working towards, it's a powerful reminder that you are capable of success and that you have the skills and resources to overcome challenges and achieve your goals.

So, how can you celebrate your successes and build your self-confidence? Here are some tips:

1. Take time to reflect: Before you start celebrating, take some time to reflect on your journey and the progress you've made. Consider the challenges you've faced, the lessons you've learned, and the skills and strengths you've developed along the way.

2. Acknowledge your achievements: Don't be afraid to give yourself credit for your accomplishments. Whether it's sharing your success with friends and family, treating yourself to something special, or simply taking a moment to pat yourself on the back, acknowledging your achievements is an important part of building self-confidence.

3. Keep a success journal: Consider keeping a journal or a list of your successes and accomplishments. This can be a powerful tool for building self-confidence, as it allows you to see your progress over time and reminds you of your abilities and strengths.

4. Set new goals: Once you've celebrated your success, it's time to set new goals and challenges for yourself. This can help you to maintain your momentum and continue building your self-confidence.

5. Share your success: Finally, don't be afraid to share your success with others. Not only does this allow you to celebrate with friends and family, but it can also inspire and motivate others to pursue their own goals and dreams.

In conclusion, celebrating your successes is an essential part of building and maintaining self-confidence. By taking the time to acknowledge your achievements, reflect on your journey, and set new goals, you can continue to build your self-confidence and achieve success in all areas of your life. So, don't forget to take a moment to celebrate your successes, no matter how big or small they may be!

Chapter 5: Finding your inner confidence
What is inner confidence?

Inner confidence is a term used to describe a deep sense of self-assurance that comes from within. Unlike external confidence, which is often based on accomplishments, possessions, or approval from others, inner confidence is rooted in a strong sense of self-worth and self-acceptance. It's the kind of confidence that allows you to face challenges, take risks, and pursue your goals with a sense of ease and trust in yourself.

Inner confidence is not something that can be achieved overnight, nor is it something that is easily measured or quantified. It's a state of being that evolves over time, as you gain more knowledge and experience, and as you learn to trust yourself and your abilities.

One of the key components of inner confidence is self-awareness. When you are self-aware, you are able to recognize your strengths and weaknesses, your values and beliefs, and your motivations and aspirations. This knowledge allows you to make informed decisions and take actions that are aligned with your true self, rather than trying to please others or live up to external expectations.

Another important aspect of inner confidence is self-acceptance. This means accepting yourself for who you are, flaws and all, and recognizing that your worth is not determined by external factors such as appearance, status, or accomplishments. When you accept yourself, you are able to approach challenges with a sense of self-compassion and self-love, rather than judgment or criticism.

Inner confidence also involves a sense of resilience and adaptability. When you have inner confidence, you are able to bounce back from setbacks and challenges, and you are able to adapt to changing circumstances with a sense of flexibility and openness. You are not afraid to take risks or try new things, because you have a deep trust in your own abilities and your ability to navigate whatever comes your way.

Overall, inner confidence is a powerful state of being that can help you to live a more fulfilling and meaningful life. It's not something that can be achieved by external measures such as wealth or status, but rather it comes from within, as you learn to trust yourself, accept yourself, and believe in yourself. In the following sections, we will explore some strategies and techniques for cultivating inner confidence, so that you can start living your life with a greater sense of ease, purpose, and joy.

How to find your inner confidence

Inner confidence is a state of mind that comes from within, independent of external validation or approval. It is a deep sense of self-assurance that is not swayed by external circumstances or the opinions of others. While building self-confidence focuses on developing confidence in one's abilities and skills, finding inner confidence involves developing a sense of self-worth and trust in oneself. Here are some ways to find your inner confidence:

1. Practice self-awareness: Understanding your thoughts, feelings, and behaviors is the first step in developing inner confidence. Take some time to reflect on your values, beliefs, and goals. Ask yourself what you stand for and what you want to achieve in life. This self-awareness will help you align your actions with your values and stay true to yourself.

2. Practice self-care: Taking care of yourself physically, emotionally, and mentally is vital for developing inner confidence. Make sure to get enough sleep, exercise regularly, eat a healthy diet, and practice relaxation techniques such as meditation or deep breathing. Self-care also involves setting boundaries and saying no to things that do not align with your values or goals.

3. Embrace your imperfections: No one is perfect, and accepting your imperfections is a key component of inner confidence. Recognize that mistakes and failures are a natural part of the learning process, and use them as opportunities to grow and learn. Embracing your imperfections also means being authentic and true to yourself, instead of trying to conform to society's expectations or the opinions of others.

4. Build a support system: Surrounding yourself with positive and supportive people can help boost your inner confidence. Seek out friends, family members, or mentors who encourage and uplift you, and who believe in your abilities and potential. This support system can help you overcome challenges and setbacks and provide you with the motivation and encouragement you need to achieve your goals.

5. Practice gratitude: Focusing on what you have rather than what you lack can help you develop a sense of gratitude and appreciation for yourself and your life. Take time each day to reflect on the things you are grateful for, and celebrate your achievements and successes, no matter how small they may seem. Gratitude can help shift your focus from self-doubt to self-acceptance and build your inner confidence.

6. Focus on your strengths: Identifying and focusing on your strengths can help you build your inner confidence. Make a list of your skills, talents, and achievements, and use them to guide your actions and decisions. Celebrate your strengths and accomplishments, and use them to fuel your motivation and self-assurance.

7. Take risks: Stepping outside of your comfort zone and taking risks can help you build your inner confidence. Embrace new challenges and opportunities, even if they scare you. Remember that failure is a natural part of the learning process and use it as an opportunity to grow and develop.

In conclusion, finding inner confidence involves developing a deep sense of self-assurance and self-worth. By practicing self-awareness, self-care, embracing imperfections, building a support system, practicing gratitude, focusing on strengths, and taking risks, you can develop your inner confidence and achieve your goals with greater self-assurance and determination.

Conclusion
The importance of inner confidence

Inner confidence is an essential component of a fulfilling and successful life. It is the foundation upon which we build our self-esteem, self-worth, and self-respect. When we possess inner confidence, we are more resilient, more determined, and more capable of facing life's challenges with grace and courage.

There are many reasons why inner confidence is crucial to our well-being. Perhaps the most important is that it allows us to be true to ourselves. When we have inner confidence, we are more comfortable expressing our opinions, making decisions that align with our values, and pursuing our passions. We are less likely to be swayed by external pressures or the opinions of others, and we are more likely to stay true to our authentic selves.

Inner confidence also helps us to build better relationships. When we are confident in ourselves and our abilities, we are more likely to attract people who respect us and appreciate us for who we are. We are less likely to settle for relationships that are unhealthy or unfulfilling, and we are more likely to form connections with people who share our values and aspirations.

Another benefit of inner confidence is that it helps us to achieve our goals. When we believe in ourselves and our abilities, we are more likely to take risks and pursue our dreams. We are less likely to be held back by fear or self-doubt, and we are more likely to persist in the face of obstacles or setbacks.

So how can we cultivate inner confidence? There are several strategies that can help. First, it is important to practice self-care. Taking care of our physical, emotional, and mental health is essential for building inner confidence. This might include things like exercise, healthy eating, meditation, therapy, or spending time with loved ones.

Another key strategy is to practice self-compassion. This means being kind and understanding towards ourselves, especially when we make mistakes or face setbacks. Instead of beating ourselves up or dwelling on our shortcomings, we can learn to offer ourselves the same kindness and support that we would offer to a friend.

Another important way to cultivate inner confidence is to practice gratitude. Focusing on the things we are grateful for can help us to maintain a positive outlook and appreciate the good things in our lives. This, in turn, can help us to build resilience and cope with challenges more effectively.

It is also important to challenge our negative self-talk. Negative self-talk is one of the biggest obstacles to inner confidence, as it can undermine our sense of self-worth and make us doubt our abilities. By practicing positive self-talk and reframing negative thoughts, we can learn to be kinder and more supportive towards ourselves.

Finally, building a strong support network is essential for cultivating inner confidence. Surrounding ourselves with people who believe in us and support us can help us to stay motivated, persevere through challenges, and maintain a positive outlook.

In conclusion, inner confidence is an essential component of a fulfilling and successful life. By practicing self-care, self-compassion, gratitude, positive self-talk, and building a strong support network, we can cultivate inner confidence and live a more fulfilling life. Remember, you are worthy, capable, and deserving of success and happiness. With inner confidence, you can achieve anything you set your mind to.

How to continue to build your inner confidence

Building inner confidence is an ongoing journey, and it requires consistent effort and practice. Here are some tips on how to continue to build your inner confidence:

1. Embrace your strengths: One of the most important things you can do to build your inner confidence is to recognize and embrace your strengths. Take the time to reflect on your unique talents and abilities, and focus on cultivating and honing these skills. When you feel confident in your strengths, you are more likely to approach challenges with a positive mindset and overcome obstacles.

2. Challenge yourself: Continuing to challenge yourself is essential for building inner confidence. Whether it's trying a new hobby, taking on a new project at work, or stepping outside of your comfort zone, taking on new challenges helps you to build resilience and confidence in your ability to handle difficult situations.

3. Practice self-care: Taking care of yourself is key to building and maintaining inner confidence. This means making time for activities that bring you joy and relaxation, getting enough sleep, eating well, and engaging in regular exercise. When you prioritize your physical and emotional well-being, you feel more confident in your ability to handle stress and challenges.

4. Surround yourself with positivity: The people you surround yourself with can have a significant impact on your inner confidence. Seek out relationships and friendships with people who support and encourage you, and who believe in your abilities. Avoid negative, toxic relationships that can undermine your self-confidence and self-worth.

5. Practice gratitude: Gratitude is a powerful tool for building inner confidence. By focusing on the positive aspects of your life and expressing gratitude for the good things you have, you can shift your mindset to a more positive, confident outlook. Take time each day to reflect on the things you are grateful for, and make gratitude a regular part of your routine.

6. Focus on the present moment: Building inner confidence requires focusing on the present moment and letting go of negative thoughts and worries about the past or future. Practice mindfulness techniques such as meditation, deep breathing, or yoga to help you stay grounded in the present and maintain a positive mindset.

In conclusion, building inner confidence is a lifelong journey that requires consistent effort and practice. By embracing your strengths, challenging yourself, practicing self-care, surrounding yourself with positivity, practicing gratitude, and focusing on the present moment, you can continue to build and maintain your inner confidence over time. Remember, building inner confidence takes time and effort, but the rewards are well worth it – a greater sense of self-worth, resilience, and the ability to face life's challenges with courage and confidence.

THE END

Wordbook

Welcome to the glossary section of this book. Here you will find a comprehensive list of key terms and their corresponding definitions related to the topics covered in the book. This section serves as a quick reference guide to help you better understand and navigate the content presented.

1. Self-confidence: A belief in one's own abilities, qualities, and judgment.

2. Self-esteem: One's overall subjective evaluation of oneself, including feelings of self-worth and self-respect.

3. Self-efficacy: One's belief in their ability to accomplish specific tasks or goals.

4. Positive self-talk: The internal dialogue a person has with themselves, including affirmations, positive statements, and encouragement.

5. Negative self-talk: The internal dialogue a person has with themselves that is critical, discouraging, and self-defeating.

6. Mindfulness: A state of being present and fully engaged in the current moment, without judgment.

7. Gratitude: The practice of expressing appreciation for the positive aspects of one's life and acknowledging the contributions of others.

8. Setbacks: Obstacles or challenges that impede progress toward a goal or achievement.

9. Resilience: The ability to bounce back from setbacks and adapt to change or adversity.

10. Inner confidence: A sense of self-assurance and belief in oneself that comes from within, rather than external validation or approval.

Supplementary Materials

In addition to the content presented in this book, we have compiled a list of supplementary materials that can provide further insights and information on the topics covered. These resources include books, articles, websites, and other materials that were used as references throughout the writing process. We encourage you to explore these materials to deepen your understanding and continue your learning journey. Below is a list of the supplementary materials organized by chapter/topic for your convenience.

Introduction

No specific references required.

Chapter 1: The importance of self-confidence

Branden, N. (1995). The Six Pillars of Self-Esteem. Bantam Books.

Chapter 2: How to build your self-confidence

Hollis, R. (2005). Finding True North: Discover Your Values, Enrich Your Life. Hyperion.

Chapter 3: Maintaining your self-confidence

Dweck, C. S. (2006). Mindset: The New Psychology of Success. Random House.

Chapter 4: Dealing with setbacks

Seligman, M. E. (1998). Learned Optimism: How to Change Your Mind and Your Life. Vintage Books.

Chapter 5: Finding your inner confidence

Brené Brown (2012). Daring Greatly: How the Courage to Be Vulnerable Transforms the Way We Live, Love, Parent, and Lead. Avery.

Conclusion

No specific references required.

www.ingramcontent.com/pod-product-compliance
Lightning Source LLC
LaVergne TN
LVHW012127070526
838202LV00056B/5899